# Surviving The Storm

S. Bright

This book is dedicated to anyone that has ever gone through something difficult. No matter whom you are or what you've been through, you are not alone. I hope these pieces help us all learn to communicate with each other so we will turn our trauma into triumph. We can and will get through this storm.

If you cannot see the light..

Be the light.

# -TIME-

My grandmother always told me

What you "can't live without"

A few years from your tears

You'll have gone a new route

After time and life lessons

You'll remember just why

That God didn't want it

And you'll never again cry

# -NOT TODAY-

Don't tell me that you love me

Don't tell me that you care

Because when I fucking needed you

You were not fucking there

Don't tell me that it's different

Don't tell me that you've changed

The fact you're really standing here

Is clearly fucking strange

Don't bring up all the good times

They don't outweigh the bad

Yes I know what you have lost

You must be fucking sad

Goodbye, this is your closure

I do not fuck with you

Wish you the best

I passed this test

I don't care what you do

# -THE DARKNESS-

I stare into darkness and wonder what resides in the light

How every window has a story to tell, or even yell through the night

I hope your homes are happy and I hope that you feel safe

I hope whatever happened never made you lose your faith

I hope your kids grow up strong in a world that's made of love

I hope that every prayer you have is answered from above

I hope you're never hungry and I hope you're not without

I hope you know how amazing you are and never have a doubt

I hope our loved ones lost in life will always live through you

I hope that we unite as one so we can push on through

I hope we cherish holidays before the nonsense and the greed

I hope that every single soul has the support system they need

But if not, it's ok, let my intentions be known

Because even if you're by yourself, my love you're never alone

# -TOXIC-

If any of you have ever met a toxic spirit, you know they do not change. They morph into anything necessary to get back into your life so they can cause trouble. Especially when you are happy. They will stop at nothing and will not be satisfied until there's nothing left of you. Then they move on to the next one. Find the strength to notice red flags so you can avoid these situations before they evolve. Do not let them take your power. That's all they want.

# -THE SHIFT-

"You don't work out hard enough"

Oh, you have no idea

Of what I've done the last six years

To get myself here

I can't believe the things you say

Now you're so mean to me

What happened has been night and day

I'm shocked, what I see

# -FORGIVE ME-

Please God forgive the mistakes that I've made
I know I was wrong from the price that I've paid
But I trust all my lessons and I have no regret
I will only try harder with the goals that I set

I pray you stay with me and guide me through this
Some days I feel stuck in a deep, dark abyss
My soul is so heavy from the pain and heartbreak
But I know I won't grow without mistakes that I make

I'm thankful for my family
I'm thankful for my life
Please bring my soul comfort as I navigate strife

# -NEVER ALONE-

If you ever feel lonely

Not matter what you believe

God will always be with you

And protect while you grieve

You can never be lonely

When you have the best by your side

No matter the struggle

God will be your life guide

Don't you ever lose focus

Keep your eyes on the plan

No matter what happens

Just do the best that you can

# -THE PAIN-

I cannot breathe
My chest feels tight
Waking up alone
Throughout the night

I'm nauseous now
This type of pain
It feels so bad
I can't explain

You lied to me
I'm so ashamed
You did me wrong
Then gave me blame

You had to go now
It was time
I can't pretend
It all was fine

I wish you well
From my broken heart
I never thought
Someday we'd part

It's for the best
The lesson's done
Now it's time
To have some fun

# -CHANGES-

I'll never forget

The lessons I've learned

How you can give someone your whole life

And still end up burned

They can tell you sweet nothings

What your heart wants to hear

Then use all your weakness

Until you're crippled with fear

I'll never forget this

The pain will subside

And someday I'll be thankful

That my spirit's not died

But for now I'm still mourning

The loss of our life

Even though you were toxic

And pierced my heart like a knife

I pray for the strength now

Please forgive my mistakes

And guide me through all this

No matter how long it will take

My life feels so lonely

But I'll always have God

I've had so many signs ignored

That now it seems odd

I'll never ignore them again

I'm now prepared for this plan

I will try to stay focused

And do the best that I can

# -THE DATE-

I went out with a guy

That didn't even try

One time I ordered 2 sushi rolls

He had the nerve to ask "why?"

Then I met the love of my life

He asked to make me his wife

He orders 4 sushi rolls

And hand feeds me, no strife

Never fucking settle

## -WHO IS THIS-

I don't like myself

Or how I feel

The pain inside

Just seems unreal

The love you gave

I never knew

It could exist

Let alone come true

A few months pass

And now you've changed

You lie and cheat

I feel deranged

The man I knew

He is not here

Who is this man

I start to fear

## -MOTHER-

From the minute you pushed me to make it through birth

For the millions of pushes to guide me on Earth

I'm thankful God blessed me with a mother like you

You have always been there to push me on through

At my weakest moments

You are there when I fall

No matter the struggle

You help me get through it all

Unconditional love

You never ask for a thing

If we ever feel down

You just make our hearts sing

With your light in my life

Things are always much better

Wishing you a happy Mother's Day

Prayers for many more together

# -HOW STRANGE-

Random thought… we live in a strange place.

A world where (ironically) light skinned people pay for melanin and dark skinned people pay for bleach treatments.

Wouldn't it be amazing if we could just love ourselves the way the world intended and not for what society tells us to do?

Also, to love and accept each other!

Who the fuck cares if someone does not look like you? I promise that's what makes them so amazing!

Go talk to them and find out!!

Oh they do not speak your language? Google translate, baby!

We condemn things we fear most.. the things we don't understand. Things that are different and fall outside of our comfort zone.

Let's start a movement. Let's get uncomfortable.

Today, I hope we choose to go against societal "norms," and love ourselves the way God intended.

Also, to love each other.

## -KEEP FIGHTING-

I love you so much!

And I hope you choose to never give up!!

I hope today you fight harder than you've ever fought in your life.. for your dreams.. for your health.. for your family!

Turn your pain into power

Train your trauma for triumph

You are amazing and you can freaking do this!

Let's go <3

# -HYPOCRISY-

We live in a world where women are expected to only thrive in a sexualized environment… then proceed to point fingers and judge the paths they chose for survival. In a world with minimal options, what a ridiculous hypocrisy. I am not condoning this lifestyle… I am not shunning. I'm simply saying that someday we will live in a world where women are equal to men. In every way, shape and form. A world where people can't tell young women to not wear tank tops because they are being sexualized by predators and society does not want them inconvenienced. I pray for the day where everyone can be recognized for what's inside their soul and not outside their body. I want a better life for my nieces. I want a better existence for your family, too. We can do this.

## -STOP-

Stop moving mountains for people throwing stones at you.

Pick up those stones and build your fucking empire.

# -MY FIRST RAP-

Think that I want you (I don't)

Just cuz you blew 100 grand

You think you're ballin' out the mud

I come from deep within quick sand

You just don't understand

Don't get it

Or maybe yet you do

Seems like you're listening to me

But the words just won't go through

Don't want your money

I can't be bought

That life is not for me

And if you try to ask again

There is a problem you will see

I've got my own empire

I'm flossin'

I'm a bossy badass bitch

And if you're ever wondering

Don't need a man to make me rich

Don't wanna hitch up

Don't want your cars

I'll buy my own Gucci

Independent stack

Your shit is wack

That life is not for me

## -NO CELEBRATION-

I do not consider myself a history buff by any means, but his year.... I will NOT celebrate Columbus Day. This year... I acknowledge the truth and speak of our past trauma so we can heal and move forward as a nation.

This country was not discovered by some clown on a boat. This country was already inhabited by wonderful Native American families that those men on that boat decided to slaughter.

They were tired of paying taxes and floated over here to create their own corrupt system. After taking advantage of these people, they murdered thousands and got what they wanted.

And now here we are... standing knee deep in the corruption, trying to survive.

This year... I pay respects to my roots. I will cherish my Native American heritage and respect the truth.

# -LET YOUR SPIRIT GO WILD-

I never knew what to look for
When finding myself
I never knew what I wanted
Aside from fixing my health

But the more that I wandered
The more my soul thrived
How did I miss this so long
I've never felt so alive

The days turned to weeks
Then to months
And now years
Every adventure I took
Slowly depleted my fears

The things that felt wrong
Are now what I love that's so right
I feel courageous and confident
The darkness succumbed to the light

If you've lost who you are
And you're not sure what to do
Spend some time with yourself
And let your greatness push through
Remember the passion you had
When you were a young, restless child
And never forget who you are
Just let your spirit go wild.

# -TAKE IT BACK-

Nearing the day
When spirits are ready to fly
You learn you can't take with you
All the stuff that we buy

You can only take with you
The love that you shared
The kindness you spread
And the memories you dared

Live life to the fullest
Don't waste one more day
Go explore things you want to
Where there's a will there's a way

Take back your own happiness
And live your best life
Don't waste your time fretting
Over insignificant strife

The things we take with us
Are what matters the most
You must cherish life fully
And stay completely engrossed

# -THE STRUGGLE-

Have you ever woke up

And wished you weren't really there

You don't want to die

But then again, don't really care

So you figure what's the next best route

To live on the edge

To not feel the pain

But not fall off the ledge

I'll drink some

Maybe a few drinks

Will make it subside

Maybe I'll feel better

And not just like I've died

It's gonna be alright sis

The things you've survived

Put on your big girl pants

It's now time to thrive

## -NOT LIKE THE REST-

One of a kind

Not saying the best

But I can tell you whole-heartedly

I am not like the rest

Broken people throw shade

So just keep pushing forward

Fill your free time with knowledge

Don't give up with you're bored

Stop letting people hurt you

They just have no right

Never forget that you're loved

And keep up the good fight

## -THE SHUT DOWN-

Every day I wake up here… I immediately want to shut down. The only thing I can think about is how I can hide from this life. I could leave this world and wouldn't be sad. I'll drink, it helps but doesn't stop the trauma from coming. My music won't play loud enough, I'll turn it up until my ears bleed. The pills feel like dying without the commitment. It hits the spot, but it's never enough. Then you wake up and do it all over again.

## -HE DOESN'T EXIST-

I have a friend you should meet

Please just give him a call

I don't understand why

You're not dating at all

Don't you want your own family

And a husband to kiss

Don't you want what you're missing

All that marital bliss

You're not living your life right

Let me go down the list

Well of course, but the man I want doesn't exist

I skip to the left and I swipe through the right

Knowin' deep down my heart doesn't feel just quite right

I've searched and I've scrolled through the boredom at night

And I'm ready for change that's a comin'

I've been through scholars and dollars

Yes, I've been down the list

But the man that I want

He just doesn't exist

Oh the man that I want simply doesn't exist

# -THE NARCISSIST-

A narcissist will do everything in their power to destroy your name after doing something terrible to you… out of fear their own name will be tarnished when darkness finally comes to light. They will stop at nothing and it's really sad.

Be thankful the world shows you the truth. And more importantly, be strong enough to stay away from toxic bullshit.

## -NO WORRIES-

Never worry about words spoken behind your back.

They were achieved by someone not brave enough to say it to your face.

# -NO ASSUMPTIONS-

If you assume you cannot succeed with limited resources just remember some of the most beautiful flowers in the world blossom through the heat of the desert sand.

Believe in yourself.

You've got this.

# -THE MISSING PIECE-

Puzzle pieces cannot do much when scattered all over the table…

It's only when they come together that we see the bigger picture.

## -THE SWAP-

Today, I hope you love yourself enough to swap out that soda for something nutritious.

I hope you love yourself enough to throw away your last pack of cigarettes and never look back.

Whatever your goal, wherever you are…

I hope you do big things for YOU today!

One of my favorite quotes is “the journey of 1,000 miles begins with a single step.”

Today, I hope you take your step.

# -GO WORK OUT-

Did you have a rough day?

GO WORK OUT

Did you have a great day? Fabulous!!

GO WORK OUT

Do you have stress piling up that you're having trouble with?

GO WORK OUT

Has anxiety or fear caused issues in your life after the chaos that was 2020?

GO WORK OUT

This year is all about YOU

A chance to be proud of yourself for surviving the odds and prove to the world that you can do this

Nobody else is in control of your happiness, nor should they.

That challenge is within you if you choose to accept it.

You've got this!

I freakin' believe in you!!

Today, exercise for a better tomorrow.

# -THE CALL-

We got an emergency phone call stating their mother was on hospice and the daughter that came to take care of her had randomly passed away in bed. She was not much older than me. Those cases always hurt most.

We never know when our time is up here so please go hug your family today.

Tell them you love them and show them how much you care.

If you're not able to see each other in person.... Make that phone call!

Click on FaceTime!!

Write a letter!!!

Stop making excuses for why you can't take time out of your day to let them know how much they mean to you.

Because when it's all said and done... the things we regret most are the chances we didn't take.

The conversations we didn't have.

And the love we didn't share.

Go love your family and friends today!

And please remember to make the most of it.

# -THE M FACE-

Your game is weak if you're still trying to see that "O" face…
show me your "M" face.

Your maxed expressions..

The one right before you cannot take anymore at the gym.

That face you put on when you're about to give Earth the
scream of the decade.

The fight of your life.

Yes, let me see that face.

## -NEVER FORGET-

Today, anything is possible.

You are amazing and you can have anything you want in this life… you just need to make a plan and fight for it.

Never give up… never surrender.

And never forget you've got this.

# -SPARK IT-

The world is still weird and I'm pretty sure we are all trying our best.

Today… I hope you choose to be kind.

To yourself and to anyone that might cross your path.

We can spark change from yesterday to create light in the darkness for a brighter tomorrow.

What better time than now?

Let's rock, baby!

## -THE SHAME-

This year has taught me many things. One of my favorite (and most bittersweet) lessons was learning about the Hispanic culture. I also learned that Latina women are an amazing force to be reckoned with.

In any culture, it seems Hispanic women are underestimated and that needs to change!

They are fierce, strong and determined.

They work full time jobs and take care of the entire family (relatives, too). They cook, clean, keep the kids healthy and they are absolutely stunning in the feminine department. I do not understand how they do it all!

Hispanic families are always there for each other. If something great happens, they celebrate. If life feels tough, they celebrate just being alive! Their food is amazing! The families are bonded! This is a group of people that work very hard and take pride in what they do. They make you think about what's important. Appreciating what life gives us, family, friends and keeping a positive attitude during trying times.

I write these words, because I feel awful about how our leaders have treated Hispanic families over the years. I'm embarrassed by the racism. These people didn't deserve it. There are awful people in every culture. In every race, religion and in every job. There are good and bad people in every aspect of life. To have the audacity of stating an entire race of people are bad, I cannot even explain how upset that makes me. I never believed those things they said and I am sorry.

I hope to learn about every type of person in my life.

Every culture and ethnicity.

I also hope someday we are all loved and accepted for who we are; human beings. Regardless of ethnicity, background, religion, job, or anything else that makes us different... we are all in this together.

Only when we figure that out will we have a wonderful world.

# -THE FLIGHT-

As I sit on this plane
And watch the people walk by
I can't help but wonder
Why they came here to fly

Are they visiting family
Will they visit their friends
Are they searching for love
Or maybe trying to mend

Are they coming for business
Is it something for class
Are they home for the holiday
Or this year will they pass

Well whatever the reason
I hope they have a good life
Whether traveling alone
Or with their husband or wife

Maybe with their family
Or that man with a cat
Or the two lovely attendants
That sat near to chat

I hope we all arrive safely
I hope this snow will soon go
I hope the captain is ready
For any scenario

Our flight is now leaving
Time to put my phone down
I shall continue these thoughts
Until we arrive in our town

# -THE CHAT-

Had a conversation with a 101 year old woman last night about how she does not believe in God. When we spoke of why, I said it seems like the majority of the world lost faith in religion. Probably because they were tired of watching it hurt people. Including myself. She said that's one of the reasons she stopped believing. Shunning people... creating war and dividing the world. Every religion believes they have the answer and only their answer is correct. Ironically, we are all praying to the same God... just go by different names and everyone has a different holy figure with a different story. We have so much in common, it's absolutely ridiculous to not utilize this. To come together with all our ethics and ideas so we can live our best life possible. Not as separate entities, but as a union of imperfect human beings trying to function on this planet.

Then we spoke of how religion is man-made and most of the things in those books are not visions from God. I do not know what you believe in, but I believe God would never spread hate throughout the world. God would never ask for your paychecks to fund mega churches or so these preachers can purchase helicopters and mansions. God would never tell you that you're going to burn in Hell for being the way they made you. We are who we are. How wonderful it will be some day when we all come together. To love and accept each other no matter what path you've walked in life. Damn, I'm ready!

## -THAT STUFF-

I read a beautiful quote by Ann Voskamp that said "Shame dies when stories are told in safe places."

That stuff you went through... you're not alone!

We have more in common than we think!!

Doesn't matter if you grew up different, look different, act different, speak different... we are all the same.

We are all human.

And you better believe we all go through things.

Life is short, let's talk about it!

# -BABY STEPS-

You can never give up!

Baby steps lead to marathon miles.

We all start somewhere.

# -PAINFUL PERFECTION-

This was the first year that I was able to control my urges for needing everything to be perfect.

As we put up the Christmas tree at my sister's house, I wanted so badly to show my nephews how to align the ornaments to resemble a Martha Stewart advertisement.

When I seen how happy it made them to place them in total anarchy, 14 deep all hanging on one corner of the tree, it made me happy and in that moment everything was in fact perfect.

Sometimes perfect is painful and I've struggled with that my entire life.

This year changed my perspective on so many things. I'm so thankful for my family and my friends. Even if we don't keep in touch every day.

My nieces and nephews teach me so much about life. About what's important and what doesn't deserve a second thought.

I hope this holiday season we all remember what we started this for. Not the presents or the food. Not the sales or materialistic things. We cannot take any of that with us. We will only have the wonderful memories we choose to make together.

This year, I hope we cherish those most.

# -ESSENTIALS-

Fall reminds us to shed the skin of our past lives and move forward to something amazing.

Something bigger, stronger and more beautiful than the year before.

Change is good.

Change is essential.

If we are not growing, we are not living life.

# -ADDICTION-

I was passed by a bunch of bikers while driving to the store. We were stuck at an intersection.. they took up two lanes, but were respectful. The energy felt like a memorial ride. When they passed again, I seen the jackets said "Sober Souls." It made me feel so many things. One of the worst pains is watching someone you love spiral from drugs, or any vice, they all serve purpose and destroy lives. They destroy families. They destroy communities. It only takes a second to lose that person and after it's said and done there's nothing you can do about it. No matter how hard you try, they will not change unless they want to. It's a powerless feeling.

We have to come up with a better system in this country. We have to develop a lifestyle that nobody wants to hide from. Where everyone has a chance to live a good life. Nobody should have to work 80 hours a week.. let alone still not be able to afford a vacation. Or even healthy groceries. Everyone should have access to healthcare that won't steal their paychecks... so they can utilize resources and fix lingering trauma causing the addictions. Everyone deserves safe access to marijuana products in case they choose to go an alternative route for pain instead of dangerous and addictive pharmaceuticals. There are so many things we can (and will) fix. We don't have to settle for the life this corrupt government deems fit. We can have any life we want. We just have to make a plan and fight for it.

If you are suffering from addiction, you're not alone. If you love someone with an addiction, you're not alone either. We have to learn how to talk about it so we can persevere.

Whatever you're going through, please stay strong.

## -GO FOR IT-

The best of life begins at the end of your comfort zone.

Stop letting anxiety or fear stop you from being the person the world needs you to be.

Stop letting it ruin your opportunities to make amazing memories.

Go for it.

And go for it with all your heart.

# -THANKFUL-

Today, I woke up thankful to be here.

Friday, I did my time at the gym. I went to lunch then decided to grab a couple lottery tickets even though I don't gamble. Leaving the gas station, I was waiting at an intersection and an uninsured drunk driver smashed into the SUV that was stopped next to me. He was going very, very fast. The impact sent the SUV through the intersection and the drunk driver hit my car. If I had pulled into that turning lane 6" to the right, he would have hit me just as hard. There is no explanation of why I'm still here or not seriously injured. I believe I had guardian angels with me. It's scary to think in one moment everything could be different and there's nothing you can do about it. We are just supposed to figure it out.

It made me think of my family and friends.. of Kansas City.

I tried my best to learn a lesson out of the chaos. I believe it was the world letting me know I have to stay focused. Also, to speak with anyone that might be going through things that feel overwhelming right now. You are absolutely not alone! Or, if for any reason, you are trying to numb your life from whatever pain you're dealing with, please do not choose to drive. There is no judgement from me, we are all going through things, but we have to figure out a way to stop all the madness.

I did not win the lottery that day, but I feel like I did.

No amount of money on this planet can save your life when it's time to go.

I am thankful to be here.

# -NIGHT BEFORE CHRISTMAS-
# (ADULT VERSION)

Twas the night
before Christmas

And all through
Kansas City

Chiefs fans slept
sound

Because the
Broncos played
shitty

The trains inside
Fritz's served
their last meal
for the night

But the lady at
Gates is still
ready to fight

The
Independence
Bridge rests it's
bones
undefeated

While the one in
Olathe takes
some notes that
are needed

The lights on the
Plaza twinkle
bright with the
snow

Bringing comfort
and joy to all the
people that go

Parents are
home wrapping
gifts and drinking
Boulevard Beer

Preparing for
Santa, for he
soon would be
here

They fill all the
stockings with

the toys from
Crown Center

And crank up the
heat for that
Kansas City
winter

It's now time for
bed, Santa will
finish the rest

If you were
naughty or nice,
he's the best at
this test

So sleep well KC,
it will be
Christmas Day
soon

Keep an eye out
for Santa as he
floats past the
moon.

## -AMAZING-

You are amazing.

You are an inspiration of infinite possibilities

Dancing through life like a leaf lost in a whirlwind.

I hope you never underestimate yourself again.

You are amazing.

# -NEGLECT-

A plant that is neglected.. not enough sunlight, the wrong nutrients, toxic environments.. will eventually wilt away and die.

I have a poinsettia plant I brought home for Christmas. Come February, it was nothing but a twig in the soil due to neglect. I was going to toss it, but someone mentioned it was worth keeping. We started to water it and I stuck it in the window, forgetting about it over the weeks. A month went by and I decided to check on the plant.. finding it was a small bush at that point with at least half dozen leaves. With a little TLC it became a large, thriving bush by summer.

What am I getting at?

If a plant is able to revive itself with a little time and some TLC, why can't we as humans take that chance on ourselves? One day at a time we will start to better our habits and live a healthier life. Mind, body and spirit replenished... just give yourself a month.

Start drinking a little more water each day... find better ways to cope with whatever situation life has brought you to. Get a little more sunlight. In a month, see your transformation.

You've got this!

## -YOU'LL NEVER BE HAPPY-

They say you'll never be happy if you can't control weight

They say you'll never be happy if you won't start to date

They say you'll never be happy unless you find a soul mate

They say you'll never be happy unless you marry, don't wait

They say you'll never be happy if you have kids too late

They say you'll never be happy until you have a locked
mortgage rate

They say you'll never be happy unless they can relate

They say you'll never be happy if you question your fate

## -START LIVING-

It's time to start living your life now
Please don't be afraid
The darkness that's rising
Will soon start to fade

Our world is dying
The people now, too
Politicians keep lying
Spreading hate into you

We're smarter than this and we must now be strong
This spiral we're in can't continue for long

## -HAPPINESS-

One day you'll wake up and not be scared
Your spirit feels life and your heart has repaired

I never thought I'd see the day
Where happiness would come my way
The kind you feel deep in your soul
It lingers and you now feel whole

## -YOUR SWEET SMILE-

I wish I would've hugged you more
And shown how much I cared
I wish I would've told you more
Because now I'm not prepared

I love you and I miss you
My days don't feel the same
I always look for your sweet smile
When I hear them call your name

I know that we will meet again
You'll protect me 'til that day
But for now I mourn my loss
I don't know what to say

# -DON'T LISTEN-

You are amazing and loved

Do you hear what I'm saying

Don't listen to haters

Or the games they are playing

# -YOUR GLOW-

I'm thankful for another day

Hope many more will come my way

But if they don't

Please always know

I pray some day you find your glow

# -WAKE UP-

What do we do

Where do we even begin

Why can't we wake up

To save this generation

Ignite the phoenix inside you

And light a fire below

You have more power inside you

That you ever will know

We're better together

Divided we fall

We must save our poor planet

Before they conquer it all

## -THE PEARL-

Some days you'll search endlessly and only be able to enjoy plane oysters.

But, once in a while, you have that day where you find a pearl. The rare, beautiful memory you will forever cherish like a fine jewel.

I'll never regret a plane oyster kind of day... they help you to truly appreciate the pearls.

# -THE VIDEO-

Last night I watched a video

And it sadly changed my life

Last night I watched a video

And it cut me like a knife

The tears rolled down

My sobbing face

Attempting not to feel disgrace

Last night I watched a video

And it sadly changed my life

# -THE WISH-

Please don't wish bad things on me
I don't wish them on you

Please don't say that you hate me
I hope your dreams come true

Don't waste your time being afraid
Of friendships that were never made

Stay wise and kind
Be an enlightened you
For we never know what they go through

Please don't wish bad things on me
I don't wish them on you

# -OBSTACLES-

A good hike is like the game of life.

It's no fun without a few obstacles.

# -THE MISSION-

I've never feared death.

That is not what bothers me.

My biggest fear is living for nothing.

Continuing to float around in this existence... not having a plan.
Not following a path. Never fulfilling the mission.

I would rather die for something than live for nothing.

# -UNITED WE STAND-

I believe in a world where people are measured by the wealth in their hearts

And not their bank accounts.

Where everyone is welcome and accepted no matter the race, gender, sexual orientation or religious belief.

A place where love trumps hate.

A country truly great

And not from false campaign promises.

We are the land of the free and home of the brave.

Not the land of the greed and home of the slave.

We are the last sliver of freedom left on this beautiful planet..

I don't know about you, but I refuse to let that go.

We've lived a life of comfort.

It's time to say enough is enough.

It's time to take this country back.

#UnitedWeStand

## -THE POWER-

Only when I'm powerless

Do you feel powerful.

# -THE BREAK-

I hope the only thing you catch today is a break.

I hope no matter what you choose to do with your day, it brings you happiness.

And I hope today is the day you start the journey for your health and well-being.

Whether it be baby steps or Olympic lunges, we will get there eventually.

# -CHAIN OF HOPE-

Today, I hope you start the chain that will change the world.

It only takes one spark to start a wildfire.

# -YOU MATTER-

Don't you ever forget
Your life matters to me
I promise things will get better
Just keep fighting and see

We all go through hard times
I believe in your strength
And I know you will make it
Troubled no matter the length

I love you, stay warm now
I'll be praying for you
For the struggles you're fighting
May the Lord get you through.

# -I'M ON MY WAY-

Drivin' alone

Eastbound on 70

Tryin' to make it home

The feeling's heavenly

I'm on my way

I'm on my way

Pass by the Legends

Oh Lord I'm almost there

Missing my family

Stop me if you dare

I'm on my way

I'm on my way

I'm gonna hold you tight

We'll find some barbecue

Tell you some stories

Oh if you only knew

I'm on my way

I'm on my way

# -PREMIUM-

If you fill up your car with premium fuel, but then go down the street and fill your personal tank with sawdust and Ovaltine.. there's a problem.

We invest in materialistic things, but then forget to invest in our bodies. They crave nutrition and we must provide for a premium quality of life.

Get some exercise.

Take that multivitamin.

Drink your water.

No more fast food.

Invest in your future.

# -PLEASE PRAY-

If you have some free time

Regardless of your views

Please pray for our country

Whomever you choose.

# -BREAKING THE CURSE-

A day without Facebook

Let me sit down and think

Of what it would be like

To not click on that link

I wonder what happens

When you don't stress that much

To meet friends in public

When staying in touch

I wonder what it feels like

To not care at all

About the drama and chaos

That flows on my wall

Oh a day without Facebook

I think that I'll try

The more that I scroll

The more life passes by.

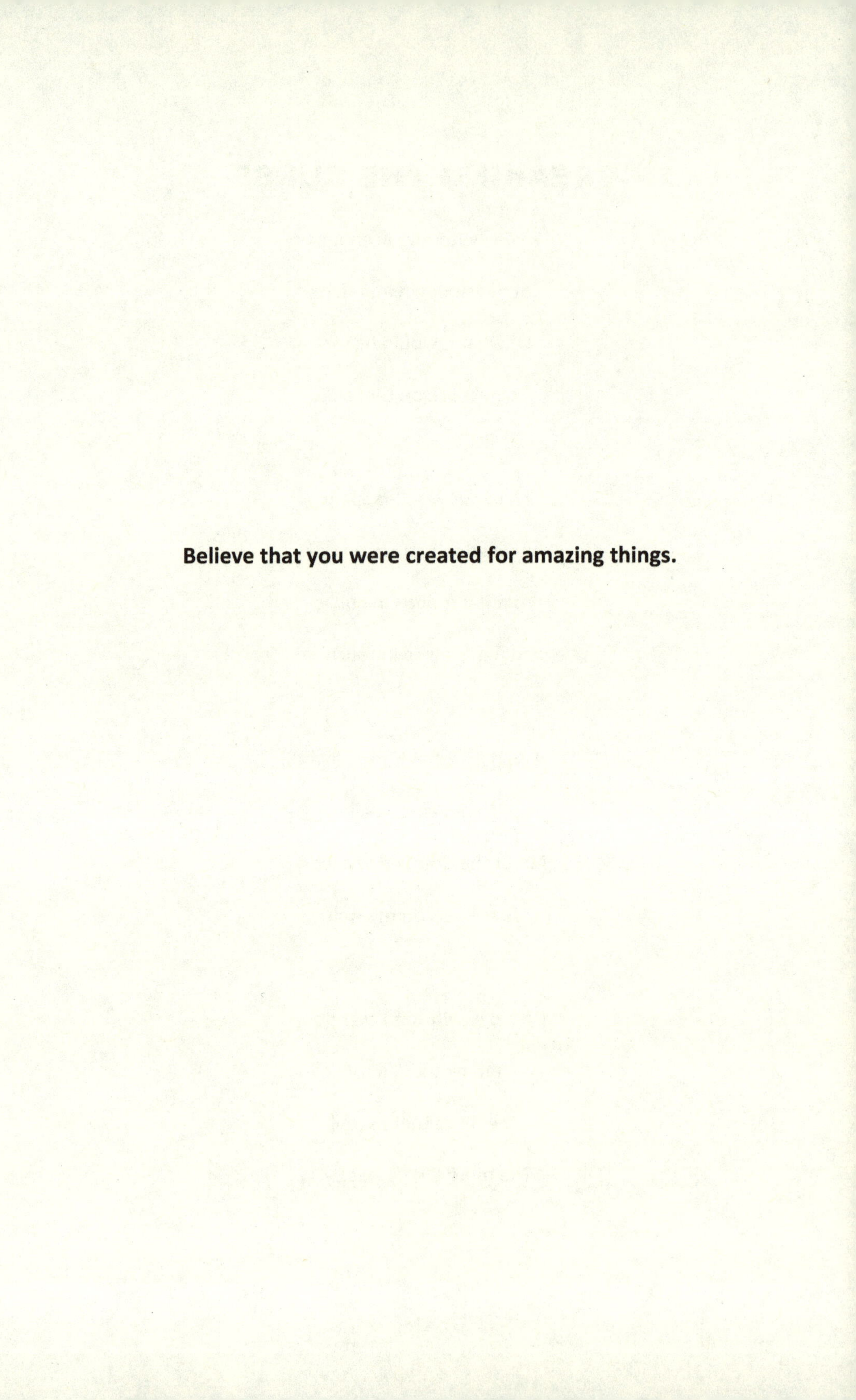

**Believe that you were created for amazing things.**

**Believe that you are enough.**

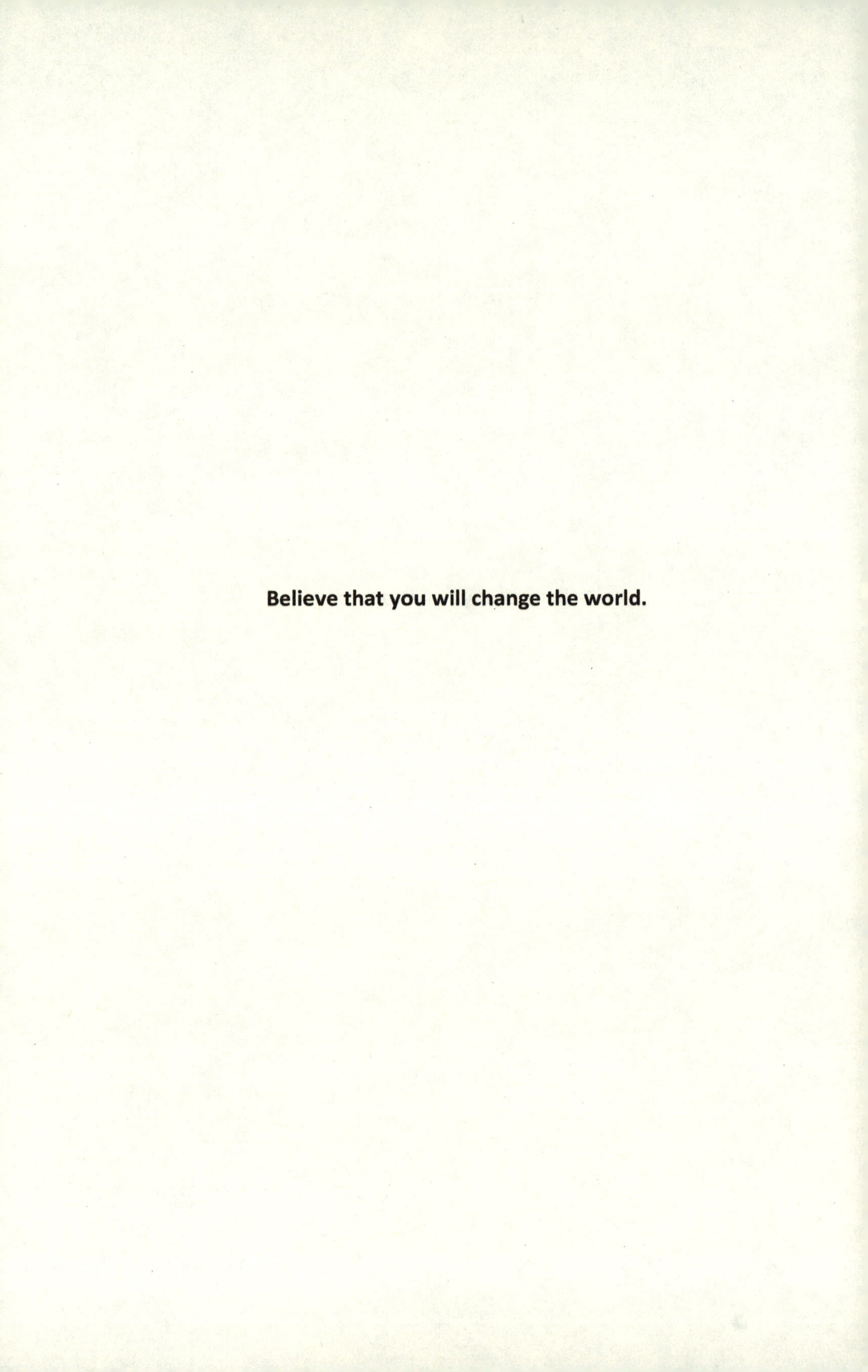

**Believe that you will change the world.**

**Always believe in yourself.**

www.ingramcontent.com/pod-product-compliance
Lightning Source LLC
LaVergne TN
LVHW041238150826
845673LV00008B/2418

* 9 7 9 8 3 6 7 8 7 4 2 4 2 *